Orion Books Ltd
Orion House
5 Upper St Martin's Lane
London WC2H 9EA

First published by Orion in 1999

Drawings by Michael Martin

Cover illustrations by Alex Graham

ISBN 0 75282 707 3

Printed and bound in Great Britain
by The Guernsey Press Limited.

ALEX GRAHAM'S FRED BASSET 1999

He's had a spot of trouble with the computer

Our local expert has been called in...

1641

...little Timothy from up the road!

TO REPLACE THE TEXT, COPY IT TO THE CLIPBOARD. CHOOSE A REPLACE COMMAND, AND IN THE FIND WHAT BOX, TYPE IN WHAT YOU WANT TO FIND...

OH, I SEE

MBM

She seems to have got the hang of this new computer

1642

It's proving very useful for her day-to-day activities

BEEP

WHIRL

She's got the neatest shopping list in the district!

MBM

IT'S ARRIVED

A vital new piece of equipment...

... to help him cope with this new computer —

1643

A joystick for his Jet Fighter game!

K-BOOM!

HELLO, BOYS—COME ON IN

THANK YOU

1644

There was a time when the Tucker twins used to call round for me, but not any more

Not since he's had that Galactic Starship Warrior game!

OK, BOYS, I'LL BE CAPTAIN COURAGEOUS AND YOU CAN BE THE ALIENS FROM THE PLANET DORK...

Thanks, Joe, don't mind if we do!

1661

I see Trevor has a hole in his sock — and look, Andrew and Sally are holding hands — how sweet

1662

Oops — somebody's dropped a potato and, would you believe it, Judith's kicking Trevor!

It's amazing what goes on under here!

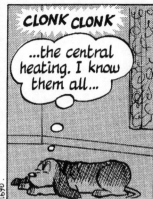

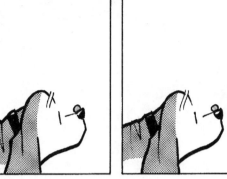

Something moved in the bushes— and Yorky has rushed in to investigate

1797

Blimey! Whatever it is, it's certainly frightened him...

...and when Yorky gets frightened, I get frightened too!

MBM

Life gets rather tedious around here sometimes—

1798

Same old routine, day in day out

DINNER, FRED

But then again, same old routines do have their moments!

MBM

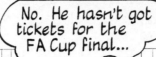